The Library of
Political Assassinations

The Assassination of
Robert F. Kennedy

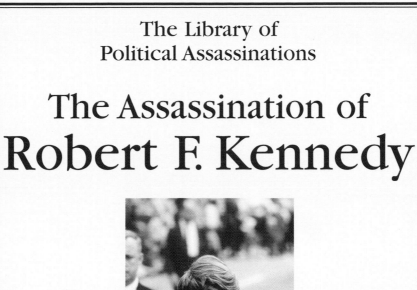

Juliet Ching

The Rosen Publishing Group, Inc.
New York

To my family

Published in 2002 by The Rosen Publishing Group, Inc.
29 East 21st Street, New York, NY 10010

Library of Congress Cataloging-in-Publication Data

Ching, Juliet.
The assassination of Robert F. Kennedy / by Juliet Ching. — 1st ed.
p. cm. — (The Library of political assassinations)
Includes bibliographical references and index.
Summary: Discusses the assassination of outspoken political
leader, his rise in politics and passion for social justice, and the
many questions that continue to linger regarding his murder and
the suspiciously botched investigation of the crime.
Summary: Discusses the assassinations of President Kennedy,
Martin Luther King, Jr., and Robert Kennedy; the investigations of
the murders; and the lingering suspicions that these crimes are
still unsolved.
ISBN 0-8239-3545-0 (library binding)
1. Kennedy, Robert F., 1925–1968—Assassination—Juvenile litera-
ture. [1. Kennedy, Robert F., 1925–1968—Assassination.]
I. Title. II. Series.
E840.8.K4 C47 2002
364.15'24'092—dc21

                                    2001004612

Manufactured in the United States of America

(*Previous page*) Robert F. Kennedy waves from a motorcade in
this undated photo.

Contents

Mrs. Ethel Kennedy gazes at a memorial to her late husband, Senator Robert F. Kennedy, following an unveiling ceremony on November 2, 1972, at Civic Center Park in Brooklyn, New York.

Introduction

The 1960s were a decade of change, when many young people found their political voices and demanded to be heard. It was also a time of turmoil, when peaceful demonstrations sometimes turned into violent confrontations between protestors and the police. The decade also witnessed the assassinations of several of the nation's political leaders. One of the most promising, outspoken, and charismatic was Robert F. Kennedy.

Robert F. Kennedy (RFK) was the seventh child of Joseph and Rose Kennedy. Bobby, as many came to call him, was an unlikely leader. As a child, he was unable to express himself very well verbally. His grades in school were not very good. Being somewhat shy did not help him to stand out in a family of nine children—four boys and five girls. Physically, he was not very coordinated. He often felt his older brothers, Joseph Jr. and John (often referred to as Jack), received much more attention from his father. In fact, Joseph Kennedy hoped that Joe Jr. would be elected the country's first Irish Catholic president; Jack, on the other hand, was considered the family intellectual.

This photo shows Robert F. Kennedy *(third from left)* with his family at their Boston home on July 8, 1934. From left to right: Edward, Jeanne, Robert, Patricia, Eunice, Kathleen, Rosemary, John, Mrs. Rose Kennedy, and Joseph P. Kennedy. Joseph Kennedy Jr., who was later killed in World War II, is not shown.

But things don't always work out as expected. Death came calling on the Kennedy family. Sadly, it turned out to be the first of many visits. In August 1944, about one year before the end of World War II, Joe Jr., a naval pilot, was killed while on a secret and highly dangerous mission over the English Channel when his bomber airplane exploded. Before his death in 1969, Joe Sr. endured the untimely deaths of three more of his children. His oldest daughter, Kathleen, died in a plane crash in southern France in 1948. His second son, Jack, who had become the thirty-fifth president of the United States, was assassinated in Dallas, Texas, in 1963. Bobby Kennedy himself was assassinated in Los Angeles, California, in 1968, ending a political career that was full of promise.

Raised by his ambitious and energetic father to be competitive, Bobby, along with his siblings, learned early that winning was everything; being second or third just wasn't good enough. His resulting focus and determination brought him success but alienated some. People who knew him well often spoke of two different Bobbys—the public one who was brash, ruthless, and seemingly opportunistic, and the private one who was compassionate, sensitive, and driven to fight social injustice. Bobby felt that "if one man's rights are denied, the rights of all are endangered." He was extremely hardworking and determined. When he made up his mind to do something, whether it was managing his brother Jack's political campaigns, fighting corruption in the Teamsters Union, or championing the rights of minorities, he threw himself into it.

The 1960s transformed the political life of Robert Kennedy. Born to a wealthy and politically liberal but morally conservative Roman Catholic, Irish American family, he was insulated from the realities of poverty and racial inequalities. As he came into greater contact with the rest of society, he

RFK ran for the presidency of the United States in 1968, the same year in which he was assassinated.

was shocked by what he saw. He witnessed people living at a level of poverty that astounded him. He saw children starving "to the point where their minds and bodies are damaged beyond repair." He saw that not all Americans were equal; some were denied the basic rights guaranteed by the Constitution.

Bobby successfully related to ordinary citizens across racial and economic lines. He arrived on the national stage at a time when those who were historically discouraged from participating in the political process—the young, the poor, and minorities—were becoming a vibrant political force. He was a candidate they could believe in. Also, as an opponent of the Vietnam War, he represented the interests of a growing portion of the population that was dissatisfied with the government's stance in Vietnam.

No longer the brother who managed events from backstage, Bobby transformed himself into the man at center stage and became a strong leader in his own right. Over the years, many continued to ask the question "What if?" What if RFK had lived to serve his country well into the next decade? Many feel his assassination ended an era of innocence during which Americans believed that the ideal of equality and justice for all could be a reality. Further, some are still troubled that the investigations into Kennedy's assassination did not do justice to his memory.

The Assassination

Tuesday, June 4, 1968: the day of the California primary. Robert Kennedy and his supporters would closely monitor the results. The American primary system is unique. Primaries enable people who are registered with the major political parties to vote for the candidate they want to represent their party in the upcoming political race. The candidate who receives the most votes wins the delegates from that state. Delegates represent state voters at a party's national nominating convention. The number of delegates each state has depends on the size of its population. There are fifty states, but in 1968, only fourteen states held primaries.

President Lyndon Johnson had removed himself from the race because of the decline in his popularity. As a result, Kennedy was running against Vice President Hubert Humphrey in the Democratic primary. Both candidates hoped to win their party's nomination for president at the national convention in August. If Democratic voters in California chose RFK over Humphrey, Kennedy would win the high number of California delegates headed to the national convention. Kennedy would become the party's candidate for president. By late evening, election results indicated that Bobby Kennedy's run for the presidency was just about to begin. But, only hours later, it came to a sudden and violent end.

The Last Days of the Campaign

On the morning of June 4, Bobby, his wife, Ethel (who was pregnant with their eleventh child), and six of their children were relaxing in the Malibu beach house of movie director and producer John Frankenheimer. It was an unseasonably cool June day. The sun hid behind clouds. Bobby and his family relaxed by the swimming pool and in the Pacific Ocean. The cool water of the ocean refreshed them. For the first time since the start of his campaign in March, Kennedy allowed himself to really let go.

It was a much-needed and well-deserved rest. The last two days before the election had passed at a crazy pace in a blur of last minute campaigning up and down California. Between June 2 and 3, Kennedy traveled 1,200 miles back and forth between San Francisco and San Diego, stopping in different cities to campaign. Jack Newfield, a journalist for the *Village Voice* who often traveled with Bobby, noted how tired and worn out Bobby looked as they flew together for this last round of campaigning. His eyes were bloodshot. His face was wrinkled like that of a man twice his age. With only two more days until the California primary, Bobby could not slow down. If he lost, there would be plenty of time for rest. He continued to make speeches before enthusiastic crowds, even though the strain was beginning to show.

Finally, on June 3, during his very last stop in San Diego, he became so physically ill that he had to interrupt his speech. The crowd there was unusually large

A Winning Streak

Kennedy *(second from right)* waits to debate Minnesota senator Eugene McCarthy *(being fitted for a microphone)* at KGO-TV in San Francisco on June 1, 1968.

Kennedy had won four out of the five primaries leading up to the California primary. He was hoping to win New York, where he was senator, two weeks later. He was pleased with his showing in South Dakota, where he won over 50 percent of the votes, because it was Hubert Humphrey's home state.

and active. In order to keep things under control, campaign organizers decided that the crowd should be split into two groups. As a result, Bobby had to make two speeches. He rushed through his first speech before he almost collapsed. He felt nauseous and was helped to the bathroom. After a few moments of rest he reemerged from the bathroom to finish the last speech of his campaign.

Waiting for the Returns

A few days before the California primary, Kennedy had been defeated in the Oregon primary by Senator Eugene McCarthy from Minnesota. His defeat there ended his winning streak and allowed him to put the possibility of a defeat in proper perspective. Having lost once, he no longer feared losing. He knew that whatever happened, he would continue his work for social justice. He wanted to "blend passion, reason, and courage in a personal commitment to the great enterprises and ideals of American society."

That afternoon, Bobby's son David, just a few days shy of his thirteenth birthday, was swimming in the ocean when a wave knocked him down. He hit his head and was dazed. Then an undertow started to carry him out to sea. Fortunately, his father swam out and brought him safely back to shore. Unfortunately, no one could save Kennedy later that night.

Kennedy arrived at the Ambassador Hotel on the evening of June 4 just after 7 PM. He and his family quickly settled into his private suite, room 511. Election results were just coming in and he was becoming a little tense. Most of his campaign staffers and various supporters and journalists were across the hallway, in room 516. The room was packed with people. Telephones rang and TV sets announced election results. Children ran around, sometimes stopping to answer telephones. The crowd was optimistic—Kennedy had just beaten Humphrey in Humphrey's native South Dakota.

By 11 PM, it was clear that Kennedy had won in California. Downstairs, at the Ambassador Hotel's Embassy Ballroom, Bobby's supporters waited anxiously for their candidate to arrive and make his victory speech. It was time for him to go.

Passage into History

About 1,800 people waited in the ballroom for Kennedy to arrive. A celebration was under way. They chanted his name and sang Woody Guthrie's ode to the promise of a just America, "This Land Is Your

Kennedy addresses a packed crowd at the Ambassador Hotel's Embassy Ballroom after his victory in the California primary. He was shot shortly after he left the podium.

Land." As Kennedy entered, the crowd clapped and cheered loudly. It had been a long evening, but the room was energized. Amid cheers of support, Bobby thanked everyone who had helped him during his campaign, including his cocker spaniel, Freckles, who had traveled with him these past months.

It was just past midnight. After the victory speech, he was scheduled to meet a group of print journalists in the Colonial Room, a small conference room next to the Embassy Ballroom. As Bobby turned away from the podium to meet with reporters in the next room, he was surrounded by a large group of his friends, campaign volunteers, reporters, and others from the audience who wanted to get a closer look at the candidate. Many crowded toward the narrow hallway leading to the kitchen pantry.

The hallway was littered with balloons from the ballroom. The rushing crowd carelessly trampled over them. The scene inside the pantry resembled a circus. Too many people were crowded into too small an area. People reached out to touch Kennedy.

As Kennedy reached out to shake the hand of a busboy, a slight young man pushed through the crowd. Facing Kennedy, he reached for his gun. He was standing about three feet away when he fired.

Witnesses claim that Kennedy first pitched forward, then backward, and then finally dropped to the ground on his back. He had been shot by Sirhan Sirhan, a twenty-four-year-old Jordanian man who had immigrated to the United States.

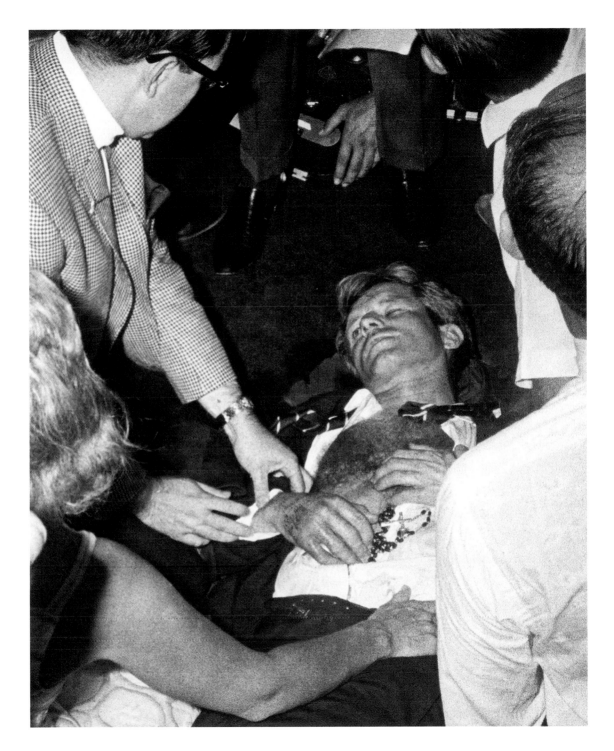

Clutching rosary beads, Kennedy lies wounded on the floor of the Ambassador Hotel after being shot following his victory speech in the California primary election. His wife Ethel *(lower left)* sits by his side.

Although several people attempted to restrain Sirhan Sirhan, he continued shooting until his gun was empty. In the end, five other people lay wounded on the ground.

Just outside the kitchen, people had heard the popping of balloons. But all of a sudden, the popping sounds intensified. Then came the sounds of men and women screaming, shouting, and crying. People inside came running out. People outside went running in.

Kennedy was rushed to the Good Samaritan Hospital for surgery, but his injuries were too extensive. Kennedy died just over twenty-five hours later, with Ethel at his side, at 1:44 AM on June 6, 1968. He was forty-two years old.

It took only a few minutes to change history. For the people who were there, every moment of that incident was etched into their memories. They would replay the minutes in slow motion and describe the events over and over to those hoping to understand what had happened.

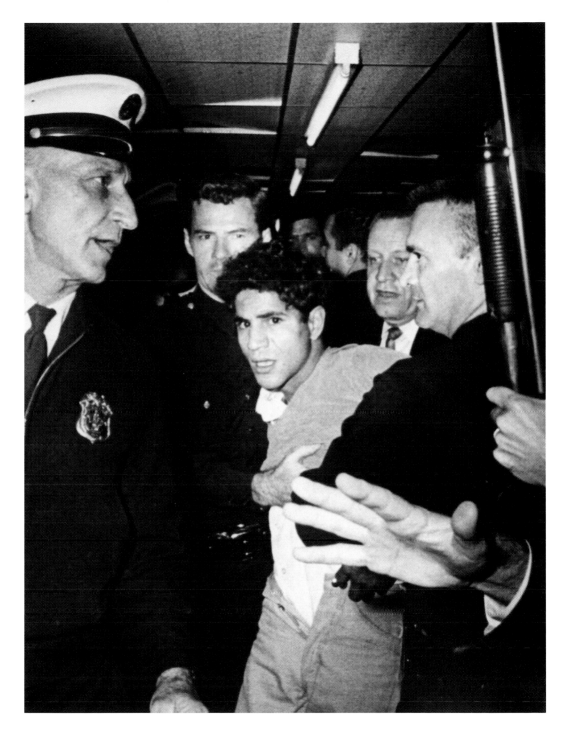

Sirhan Sirhan is lcd away from thc Ambassador IIotcl aftcr shooting
Robert F. Kennedy.

The Road to Destiny

When Robert Kennedy decided to run for president months earlier, in March 1968, many wondered why he had waited so long. After all, wasn't it manifest destiny? Didn't Jack step in when Joe Jr. was killed? Wasn't it Bobby's turn now that Jack was gone? During days of indecision, Bobby often remembered the inscription on the cigarette box that Jack had given him in 1960. It said simply, "When I'm through, how about you?"

Many unanswered questions had lingered in Bobby's mind. Was the 1968 election the right time? Should he wait until 1972? He was still quite young, only forty-two. His brother, John F. Kennedy, was just one year older when he was elected, becoming the youngest elected president in American history. He also wondered if he had enough support to beat the current president, Lyndon Baines Johnson, since an incumbent is traditionally difficult to beat. If he lost now, how would it affect his chances in the future? It was well known that Kennedy and Johnson did not get along. Would his bid for the presidency appear to be inspired by animosity? As it turned out, Kennedy ran against Johnson for only fifteen days before

President Lyndon B. Johnson *(left)* and Robert Kennedy sit in the president's car at LaGuardia airport in Queens, New York, before flying to Washington, D.C., on October 15, 1964.

Johnson stepped down from his candidacy in favor of Vice President Humphrey. Also, if he ran for president, Kennedy knew he would have to take a public stand on the bitterly divisive issue of the Vietnam War.

Bedford-Stuyvesant: A Place Called Home

Kennedy's political career took off in 1964 when he won a United States Senate seat in New York. Like senator and former first lady Hillary Rodham Clinton, he received some criticism for not being originally from New York. But, like Clinton, he won anyway.

Attorney General Robert Kennedy is surrounded by children as he walks down a street in New York City while visiting a summer reading program in Harlem. The poverty and desperation in African American neighborhoods shocked Robert F. Kennedy. He did not expect that a country as wealthy and prosperous as the United States would allow its citizens to suffer.

Kennedy took his job seriously. He would walk through the poorer and often crime-ridden neighborhoods of New York City. What he saw appalled him; he did not expect to see such severe poverty in a wealthy and developed nation like the United States. One place in particular got to him: a neighborhood in Brooklyn called Bedford-Stuyvesant, or Bed-Stuy. The neighborhood was predominantly African American. Unemployment and delinquency rates were high. Sadly, Bed-Stuy had the highest percentage of infant deaths in the country. Many residents remarked that they might as well be homeless since they often lived in condemned buildings with no heat or electricity.

When Kennedy met with the residents of Bed-Stuy in February 1966, he met a group of angry people. They were angry because their neighborhood was falling apart. Government agencies and politicians had long neglected their requests for help. For ten years, many had applied for government help at both state and federal levels. Each time they had been denied.

Kennedy made improving Bed-Stuy his top priority. His solution was to apply to the private sector for help. In spite of resistance, both from the government and some community members, he attracted businesses and brought social services to an area that many had abandoned. He helped establish two private, nonprofit organizations. One was composed of community leaders, called the Bedford-Stuyvesant Restoration Corporation, which provided the leadership for the development of the area. Through his personal contacts, he also established the Bedford-Stuyvesant Development and Services Corporation, which was in charge of fund-raising.

Kennedy's activism on behalf of the poverty-stricken complemented his support for civil rights. As he said in a speech in 1966, "Each time a man stands up for an ideal, or acts to improve the lot of others, or strikes out against injustice, he sends a tiny ripple of hope . . . these ripples will build a current which can sweep down the mightiest walls of oppression and resistance." RFK had a talent for reaching out to people who had long since given up on the government. Because he believed that change was possible, people that he touched became convinced that, yes, things could be better.

Robert F. Kennedy

March 9, 1938
The Kennedy family moves to England upon Joseph Kennedy's appointment as the first Irish American and the first Roman Catholic to be ambassador to England.

September 16, 1948
Robert F. Kennedy enters law school at the University of Virginia.

June 6, 1952
Robert F. Kennedy manages the Senate campaign of his brother, John F. Kennedy.

November 20, 1925
Robert F. Kennedy is born the seventh of nine children to Rose and Joseph Kennedy in Brookline, Massachusetts.

June 10, 1948
Robert F. Kennedy graduates from Harvard University.

June 17, 1950
Robert F. Kennedy marries Ethel Skakel in Greenwich, Connecticut.

January 14, 1953
Robert F. Kennedy works for Senator Joseph McCarthy on the Senate Permanent Subcommittee on Investigations.

February 1957—
Robert F. Kennedy is appointed
chief counsel to the Senate
Select Committee on Improper
Activities in the Labor or
Management Field (also known
as the Rackets Committee).

—**December 16, 1960**
Robert F. Kennedy is
appointed U.S. attorney
general by his brother,
President John F.
Kennedy; he serves for
three years.

November 3, 1964—
Robert F. Kennedy is
elected U.S. senator
from New York state.

—**March 16, 1968**
Robert F. Kennedy
announces his candidacy
for president of the
United States.

June 5, 1968—
Robert F. Kennedy is shot by
Sirhan Sirhan in the kitchen
pantry of the Ambassador Hotel
in Los Angeles after winning the
California primary.

—**June 6, 1968**
Robert F. Kennedy dies at
Good Samaritan Hospital
at 1:44 AM after efforts to
revive him fail.

President Johnson: The Incumbent

The animosity between Robert Kennedy and Lyndon Johnson ran deep. Johnson had served as vice president during John F. Kennedy's presidential administration and had assumed the presidency after JFK was assassinated. When Johnson served as vice president, he believed that JFK relied too much on his brother's advice. Johnson came to resent Bobby's influence; he felt that JFK should have consulted him, not Bobby.

President Johnson glances at the camera as he and his guests watch the closing session of the Democratic Convention in Atlantic City, New Jersey, on August 27, 1964. From left to right: Ethel Kennedy, Robert F. Kennedy, Mrs. Ladybird Johnson, the president, Mrs. Hubert Humphrey, Luci Johnson, and Lynda Johnson.

When President Kennedy was shot on November 22, 1963, Johnson was quickly sworn in as the new president. On the day after the shooting, when Bobby came into the Oval Office and saw boxes of Jack's papers on the floor, it was just too much for him to bear. Then he saw Johnson, by now President Johnson, come in. He lost all control and screamed at him, telling him to get out. This incident only heightened the feelings of ill will between the two men.

After the assassination of President Kennedy, President Johnson served out the term and went on to win the 1964 election, beating Republican candidate Barry Goldwater by the biggest margin in American history. At that time, his approval rating reached almost 80 percent. But then President Johnson's popularity with the American public began to decline, gradually but steadily. By the end of March 1968, it had dropped to 36 percent, in large part because of the Vietnam War.

The War in Vietnam

A country located in Southeast Asia, Vietnam was once a colony of France. It was divided into North and South in 1954. Ho Chi Minh was a Communist leader who had led the fight for independence from France. He controlled North Vietnam. During the Eisenhower administration (1953-1961), America had committed itself to helping South Vietnam hold off the North Vietnamese forces. President Eisenhower had also helped install a pro-Western leader named Ngo Dinh Diem (who had supported the French) to govern South Vietnam. Communist-backed forces, the Viet Cong, sought to take control of the government in South Vietnam. In the 1960s, the United States became increasingly involved in Vietnam, sending money, arms, and troops in support of the South Vietnamese government.

Unlike President Johnson, who never questioned American intervention in Vietnam, Senator Robert Kennedy became convinced that it was a war the United States could not win. He had always had a well-developed sense of right and wrong. To him, poverty was wrong. Racial injustice was wrong. And he came to believe that the war in Vietnam was wrong. He felt that the young people of America "see us willing to fight a war for freedom in Vietnam, but unwilling to fight with one-hundredth the money or force to secure freedom in Mississippi or Alabama or the ghettos of the North." He also felt that the war might be "doomed from the start."

In February 1966, Senator Kennedy finally took a public stand regarding Vietnam by suggesting that the United States should open peace talks with North Vietnamese forces. Kennedy's speech angered Johnson, as it was critical of his foreign policy decisions. He felt that, once again, Kennedy was questioning his judgment. For the sake of his political career, Kennedy decided not to speak publicly again about the Vietnam War.

Members of the National Guard brandish rifles against peaceful antiwar demonstrators in People's Park in Berkeley, California, in June 1969.

As the war continued to escalate, or increase in intensity, Kennedy realized he could no longer remain silent. He felt that the United States was fighting a losing battle. American troops could not overcome the guerrilla tactics of the Viet Cong. The Viet Cong fighters dug tunnels beneath villages and hid in the dense tropical foliage. American forces often had difficulty distinguishing between civilians and soldiers. They sometimes destroyed whole villages, killing the villagers, including women and children. To many, the United States seemed to be fighting a gruesome and unnecessary war.

A Troubled
Administration

President Johnson was *Time* magazine's
Man of the Year twice—in 1964 because he
was so popular, and in 1967 because he was
so unpopular. The 1967 *Time* cover showed
a caricature of Johnson much beaten down
by his troubles, a complete contrast to the
traditional portrait used for the 1964 cover.

On March 2, 1967, speaking before the Senate,
Kennedy proposed that if the North Vietnamese
agreed to peace talks, the United States should cease
bombing Vietnam. Again, Johnson took this proposal as
a personal affront. But by this time, Johnson's political
support was eroding and his public popularity rating

was dropping. More and more people, especially the young, protested against the war on college campuses and in the streets across America.

The Decision to Run

During the 1968 presidential campaign, the first primary election took place in New Hampshire on March 12. At that time, Kennedy was in California lending his support to César Chávez, the leader of the United Farm Workers (UFW) union. Kennedy had seriously considered a run for the presidency months earlier, as public opinion continued to shift against President Johnson. Then, in the New Hampshire primary, the antiwar candidate, Senator Eugene McCarthy of Minnesota, beat President Johnson, winning with 42 percent of the vote.

The stage was set. On March 16, 1968, standing in the Senate caucus room where his brother had declared his candidacy in 1960, Kennedy announced his intention to run for president:

> ... I run to seek new policies, to close the gap between black and white, rich and poor, young and old ... I do not lightly dismiss the dangers and difficulties of challenging an incumbent president; but ... At stake is not simply the leadership of our party or even our country—it is our right to moral leadership on this planet.

On March 31, in a nationally televised speech, President Johnson shocked the nation with the following words: "I shall not seek, and I will not accept, the nomination of my party for another term as your president."

Kennedy believed that life was made up of "numberless diverse acts of courage." Courage, some might call it defiance, was the one thing he did not lack. Whatever the challenge, he always met it head-on—the more dangerous the better, whether it was shooting the rapids in a kayak, overcoming his fear of horses, or running for president. He said, "Few will have the greatness to bend history itself; but each of us can work to change a small portion of events, and in the total of all those acts will be written the history of this generation."

The Enemies Without

During the course of his service to the country, Bobby had made many loyal friends and followers, but also just as many enemies and detractors. According to long time friend Arthur Schlesinger, when Bobby received news of his brother's assassination, he said, "There's so much bitterness. I thought they'd get one of us . . . I thought it would be me." Security was always an issue. Although he had received numerous pieces of hate mail while campaigning, he steadfastly refused to be surrounded by bodyguards, allowing only one, Bill Barry, a former Federal Bureau of Investigation (FBI) agent.

Conflict in the Middle East

According to the police reports, Sirhan Sirhan shot Kennedy because of the candidate's pro-Israel declarations. The conflict in the Middle East between Israelis and Arabs had been going on for decades. It was headline news in the 1960s, as it is today.

This group of Israeli soldiers prepares for battle during the Six-Day War. When the fighting ended on June 10, 1967, Israel had won an area of land equivalent to four times the size of its territory in 1949.

Palestine was the name the ancient Romans gave to an area that was occupied by Jewish and Arab people for thousands of years. After World War I, the area came under the control of Great Britain until 1947. There had never been a formal state in Palestine until the establishment of Israel in 1948 after the Arab-Israeli War. The city of Jerusalem was then divided into two—West Jerusalem went to Israel and East Jerusalem, including the West Bank, went to Jordan.

In 1964, the Palestinian Arabs, who lived in different countries all over the Middle East, decided to consolidate their political efforts into one organization, the Palestine Liberation Organization (PLO), in order to fight for the establishment of a Palestinian state. In 1967, the Six-Day War broke out between Israel and several Arab states. At the end of the six days, Israel claimed from Jordan East Jerusalem and the West Bank.

Sirhan Sirhan was a Palestinian born in Jerusalem on March 19, 1944. He immigrated to the United States when he was twelve years old. While Kennedy's pro-Israel statements made him a target of Sirhan's hatred, Kennedy was not alone in his pro-Israeli stance. It was the official policy of the U.S. government not to favor one nation over another in the sale of military weapons. But in an effort to protect American defense interests in the region, U.S. policy sometimes favored Israel and supported its military endeavors.

Fighting Against Corruption

Those who reject the notion that Sirhan acted alone feel that there were more compelling reasons for the assassination. Kennedy made several powerful enemies while he was working for the Senate in the 1950s. At that time, the United States was in the grip of a Communism scare. Two of the largest countries in the world had undergone Communist revolutions: the Soviet Union in 1917 and China in 1949. The United States is a capitalist democracy. Communism supports government ownership of property and limited individual freedoms, among other things, and thus is in opposition to capitalism.

Senator Joseph McCarthy, a friend of Kennedy's father, Joseph Sr., had just formed a committee known as the Permanent Subcommittee on Investigations. At the urging of his father, RFK went to work for McCarthy as the assistant counsel.

While the committee's aim of keeping Communism from establishing a presence in the United States was somewhat vague, its methods were fierce. Unfortunately, the committee used whatever means available, including slander and intimidation, to ruin the lives of many innocent people suspected of having Communist sympathies. For instance, many innocent people in the film industry were blacklisted as Communists or as Communist sympathizers.

Consequently, many studios refused to hire them. Some would never work again. Not surprisingly, this period is commonly referred to as the witch-hunt of the 1950s. Bobby worked over a year and a half before quitting because of bitter clashes with chief counsel Roy Cohn over the unethical tactics used by Cohn.

Kennedy later rejoined the committee after a change in leadership. In 1957, he was appointed the chief counsel of the subcommittee. As such, he concentrated on fighting corruption within the Teamsters Union and formed the Senate Rackets Committee. The full name of the Teamsters is the International Brotherhood of Teamsters (IBT). Most of its members work in the freight industry. The largest employer today of Teamster members is United Parcel Service (UPS).

The Teamsters were the largest and most powerful labor union at the time. The union was supposed to represent its working-class members and fight for fair treatment from big corporations. Instead, union management was getting richer and more powerful at the expense of its members. The Teamsters had become just another big corporation taking advantage of workers. Furthermore, the union had connections to organized crime. Members feared violent retaliation if they filed any complaints.

Robert Kennedy speaks with labor leader Jimmy Hoffa. As chief counsel for the Senate Rackets Committee, Kennedy investigated Hoffa's ties to organized crime. Hoffa mysteriously disappeared in July 1975 and was declared legally dead in 1983.

The president of the Teamsters, Jimmy Hoffa, was the main target of the Rackets Committee's investigations. Kennedy and his family started receiving death threats and noticed cars driving slowly by their house. In spite of this, Kennedy continued his investigations and eventually charged Hoffa with misappropriating $9.5 million in union funds. In 1960, Kennedy published *The Enemy Within,* an account of his investigation. He sent Hoffa a copy of the book with the inscription: "To Jimmy. I'm sending you this book so you won't have to use union funds to buy one. Bobby."

The War at Home

Some people believe that Kennedy was assassinated because of his Vietnam War agenda. The Vietnam War was being fought on two fronts. Overseas, young men were fighting the Viet Cong in South Vietnam, who had the help of the Communists in North Vietnam, China, and the Soviet Union. On the home front, protestors demonstrated against a war they thought was senseless. They wanted to bring American soldiers home. By 1968, the number of American soldiers in Vietnam had grown to half a million. In fact, George Skakel, Ethel Kennedy's nephew, was killed in Vietnam just weeks before he was scheduled to come home.

American involvement in Vietnam increased in August of 1964 when the U.S. destroyer *Maddox* was apparently attacked by the North Vietnamese in the Gulf of Tonkin, which is part of the South China Sea bordering North Vietnam. President Johnson then began an all-out effort to fight the Communist forces. He ordered the bombing of North Vietnam and sent more troops to South Vietnam. By the end of 1967, the public was led to believe that the United States had the upper hand and that the war would soon end.

The event that turned the tide of public opinion against the war came on January 30, 1968. It was the day of the Vietnamese New Year, called Tet. In celebration of this day, North Vietnam, South Vietnam, and the United States had called a brief stop to the war. But to everyone's surprise, the North Vietnamese launched a massive attack, later known as the Tet Offensive. They even invaded the U.S. embassy. Based on the images of the war on television, Americans understood that the war was far from over. They began to see the war in a different light: The United States was not, as the government told them, winning the war but losing it. Many wanted American soldiers to come home.

Robert Kennedy's antiwar beliefs made him popular with antiwar voters, especially college students, who demonstrated against the war on college campuses across the country. Others, however, including President Johnson, FBI director J. Edgar Hoover, and the defense industry, had a pro-war agenda. They wanted the war to continue, not only because they thought Communism must be held back at any cost but also because many people benefited financially from the sale of weapons. They did not want to see Kennedy elected president. A Kennedy triumph would threaten their plans.

Bobby had other prominent and powerful enemies. One in particular was Richard Nixon, who had made a bid for the presidency in 1960 but lost to Bobby's brother, John. In 1963, on the day that President Kennedy was shot, Nixon had just flown from Dallas into New York City and told the *New York Times*, "I am going to work as hard as I can to get the Kennedys out of there. We can't afford four more years of that kind of administration." By 1968, Nixon was the leading Republican candidate.

Grief and Suspicion

D r. Martin Luther King Jr. was assassinated only months before Robert Kennedy. Angry mobs rioted in cities across the nation in response to the killing of Dr. King. But there were no riots for Bobby. People were in shock. Many felt too much grief and too much disbelief. Kennedy was their hope for change and for the future. Now that was gone.

The Funeral

Bobby's funeral was held in St. Patrick's Cathedral in New York City. After the funeral, a train carried Kennedy's body to Arlington National Cemetery, located just outside of Washington, D.C.

The railroad honored him by canceling all north-bound trains. The train moved slowly south. All along the way, on the station platforms, people stood in tribute and to bid a final farewell to their hero. When the train finally arrived in Washington, it was after 9 PM. Arrangements had to be made for a nighttime funeral, the only one ever at the cemetery. Floodlights lit up the grave site, and 1,500 candles were passed out to mourners. Kennedy was buried near his brother, John.

Robert F. Kennedy Jr., son of Robert F. Kennedy, leads the pallbearers as they carry his father's casket to the grave site at Arlington National Cemetery in Arlington, Virginia, on June 8, 1968.

The Investigation

In 1968, it was not a federal crime to kill a presidential candidate, so the Los Angeles Police Department (LAPD) had jurisdiction over the investigations, instead of the FBI. Some questioned whether a police department had the resources to conduct a thorough investigation.

Conspiracy theorists, people who thought Sirhan was not acting alone, pointed out problems with the handling of physical evidence and the evidence gathering process. They thought that Sirhan was merely being used by more powerful people who wanted Kennedy out of the way.

Further complicating the investigation were reports that Kennedy had decided to travel through the hotel pantry at the last minute. But, according to Professor Philip H. Melanson, director of the Robert F. Kennedy Assassination Archives, Kennedy had planned to take that route. If Kennedy had decided to travel through the hotel kitchen at the last minute, it might suggest that the shooting was a random act. But Kennedy only reversed the very route he had traveled hours earlier on his way to the Embassy Ballroom. This would have enabled his assassin(s) to anticipate his whereabouts.

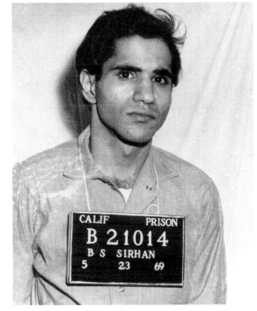

Sirhan Sirhan poses for a mug shot in San Quentin Prison in California, on May 23, 1969.

Physical Evidence

The police discovered incriminating evidence in the house where Sirhan lived with his mother. In Sirhan's bedroom, investigators found a notebook with pages of his writing, some of which detailed his obsession with killing Kennedy. He had also repeatedly written "RFK must die." After the shooting, Sirhan was in a state of disorientation, and he later claimed at his trial that he did not remember anything about the shooting.

At a hearing on August 2, 1968, soon after his arraignment, Sirhan entered a plea of not guilty. The trial did not begin until January 7, 1969, in the Hall of Justice in Los Angeles. The sitting judge, Herbert V. Walker, had a reputation of being fair but also strict. Given Judge Walker's background, the defense counsel offered a plea bargain to Sirhan just after the start of trial: change his plea to guilty in exchange for life imprisonment rather than run the risk of getting a death sentence.

On this page from Sirhan Sirhan's notebook, dated May 18, 1968, he writes of his increasing obsession with eliminating Robert F. Kennedy. Sirhan repeatedly writes, "RFK must be assassinated."

Unfortunately, Judge Walker overruled this option and ordered the trial to continue. In doing so, he was sensitive to the public's demand for the truth. The only way to get the truth, or so he thought, was to have a trial and therefore an opportunity to examine the evidence

At the trial, the defense produced psychiatric testimony indicating that Sirhan behaved like a person under hypnosis. The defense also showed that Sirhan had sustained head injuries two years earlier that would have made him vulnerable to hypnosis. The defense's strategy was not to plead outright innocence—after all, Sirhan did shoot Kennedy. The defense wanted to avoid the death penalty and show that Sirhan was not in his right mind, and was perhaps a subject of hypnosis. During his testimony, Sirhan himself admitted he might have gone temporarily insane.

Conspiracy theorists like to suggest that there might have been more than one shooter and more than one planner. There was a group of people seen with Sirhan near or on the day of the crime who the police never pursued. An Iranian man named Khaiber Khan had volunteered in Kennedy's campaign office in Los Angeles for four days just before the assassination. As it turned out, Khan was an international secret agent who had worked with the Central Intelligence Agency (CIA), especially during the CIA-backed overthrow of the Iranian government in 1953. Although not a volunteer at Kennedy's campaign office, on June 2, 1968, Sirhan had been seen there with Khan.

Sirhan had also been seen at the Ambassador Hotel with a woman in a polka-dot dress on the evening of the assassination. Other people had seen Sirhan with her earlier in the day at a shooting range. On both occasions, they were accompanied by another unidentified man. Witnesses reported seeing this woman at the Ambassador on the night of the assassination. As she left the hotel, she was heard to say with a smile on her face, "We shot him."

The third person who might have been involved in the shooting was security guard Thane Cesar, who was standing just behind Kennedy when he was shot. A witness saw Cesar pull out his gun and fire at Sirhan. But others think that he shot Kennedy instead because his position allowed him to shoot at an angle and a distance that would match up with the crime report analysis of the bullet holes.

Conviction

The trial lasted fifteen weeks, but the jury needed only three days of deliberation to return a guilty verdict. Sirhan was eventually sentenced to death for the murder of Robert Kennedy. Luckily for him, the sentence was commuted to life in prison in 1972 when California's death penalty was ruled unconstitutional. Thirty years after the assassination, Sirhan's lawyer, Lawrence Teeter, issued a statement summarizing the problems with the physical evidence.

✪ Sirhan's gun was in the wrong position to have caused Kennedy's injuries as described in the autopsy report, which showed that Kennedy was shot from behind from no more than three inches away whereas Sirhan was standing in front at a distance of at least one and one-half feet.

✪ A would-be suspect, security guard Thane Cesar, was standing just behind Kennedy and was seen firing his gun, but his gun was never checked.

✪ A fifteen-year-old named Scott Enyart took ten pictures inside the kitchen pantry during the incident; his camera was taken by the police and the photographs were never returned. Over 2,000 other assassination-related photographs were burned by the Los Angeles police in an incinerator at a county hospital.

✪ The prosecuting attorneys withheld the autopsy report from the defense counsel for four months.

✪ A door frame with two bullet holes was removed from the kitchen pantry of the Ambassador Hotel by the police, and later burned.

✪ Evidence comparing markings at the base of the bullets suggests that the police substituted bullets recovered from Kennedy's body and replaced them with those that matched bullets fired from Sirhan's gun.

✪ According to expert testimony based on pretrial examination of Sirhan Sirhan, he was probably acting under hypnosis.

The fact that conspiracy theories continue to thrive after such a long time is to a large extent due to the sloppy management of the case by the LAPD, and its insistence on keeping all the files on the case secret from the public. An example of this misman-agement is the missing door frame. Shortly after the trial, the *Los Angeles Free Press* printed an article about the existence of photographs that showed the bullet holes. When asked about this, Assistant Police Chief Daryl Gates said that the door frame had been X-rayed, found to contain no evidence, and then burned. When asked about the X rays, he answered that they, too, had been disposed of. In spite of what seemed like outrageous incompetence at best, and a conspiracy at worst, no one at the police department was ever held responsible.

Sirhan Sirhan Seeks a New Trial

Lawrence Teeter had prepared his list in anticipation of Sirhan's bid for parole in 1997. Sirhan claimed there was new evidence in the case that would establish his innocence, but the parole board refused to hear it on the grounds that the parole hearing was not going to be turned into a new trial. At the hearing, Sirhan asserted his innocence, which contradicted his admission of guilt at the 1968 trial. He claimed that the state had engaged in an "out-and-out frame-up." He continued to maintain that he could not remember what happened and could not explain why he had been carrying a gun. This was his tenth attempt to get parole; it was rejected.

As a result, Lawrence Teeter filed a petition at the state court for a new evidentiary hearing, which would in effect lead to a new trial. Again, this was rejected. Then, in May 2000, Teeter brought the case to the California Supreme Court, which also ruled against Sirhan. Undaunted, Teeter brought the case to federal court in Los Angeles the very next day. Sirhan had been in prison for over thirty years, and Teeter felt it was time for him to be released. By March 2001, Sirhan had altogether been denied parole fourteen times. At the last parole hearing in March, he refused to attend the hearing because he knew he had no chance of release. Sirhan is currently serving time in Corcoran State Prison in central California.

After the Loss

Many things changed after the assassination of Robert Kennedy in June 1968. Republican Richard Nixon was elected president that following November. His administration would go on to determine the course of American involvement in the Vietnam War and further disillusion many Americans. More and more, the nation's citizens questioned the integrity of government officials and their motives. Not surprisingly, these years became known as the Vietnam era. For many, this era came to represent loss—the loss of lives and the loss of innocence.

The Chicago Convention of 1968

American involvement in the Vietnam War was a hot issue for both Republican and Democratic presidential candidates during the 1968 presidential campaigns. Democrat Hubert Humphrey was a pro-war candidate, while his fellow Democratic candidates, Robert Kennedy and Eugene McCarthy, were so-called peace candidates. After his defeat in the California primary,

An unidentified protestor is led away during the 1968 Democratic National Convention in Chicago. Government officials called in the army and the National Guard to suppress protests against the Vietnam War.

McCarthy lost his momentum. And then Kennedy was shot. The way was clear for Humphrey to win the presidential nomination at the Democratic National Convention in Chicago. And he did. Thousands of anti-war activists then took to the streets in angry protest.

The rioting in the streets and parks of Chicago in August 1968 lasted five days. Television coverage brought the melee into the nation's homes. The Chicago police, the army, the National Guard, and even the FBI, altogether numbering some 28,000 strong, used whatever means—tear gas, mace, raw force—to control the crowds. By the time it was over, the police had injured protestors, reporters, and innocent bystanders.

Antiwar Protests Escalate

Initially, the first antiwar protests, which started in the spring of 1965, were nonviolent demonstrations on university campuses called teach-ins. But confrontations between the protestors and the police became more heated as more troops were sent to Vietnam. Police violence at the Chicago convention changed the attitude of many protestors. They began to see the police as a violent enemy against which they must defend themselves.

One of the most violent protests occurred on May 4, 1970, after President Nixon announced on April 30 on live television a full-scale bombing of Cambodia. Until then, the Cambodian leader, Prince Sihanouk, had tried to keep a neutral stance between the Americans and the Communists in his country. This had been successful at keeping an all-out war between the Communists and the Americans from breaking out in Cambodia.

The news of the attack upset many people because it was an indication that the war overseas was intensifying. Students at Kent State University in Ohio gathered to protest the bombing. The National Guard was called in. Even though no one was armed and most protestors stood at least 100 feet away, the National Guardsmen suddenly started shooting into the crowds for a full thirteen seconds. Eight people were hurt. Two of four people killed were students who had simply been walking across campus on their way to classes. In spite of public outcry, no one was prosecuted.

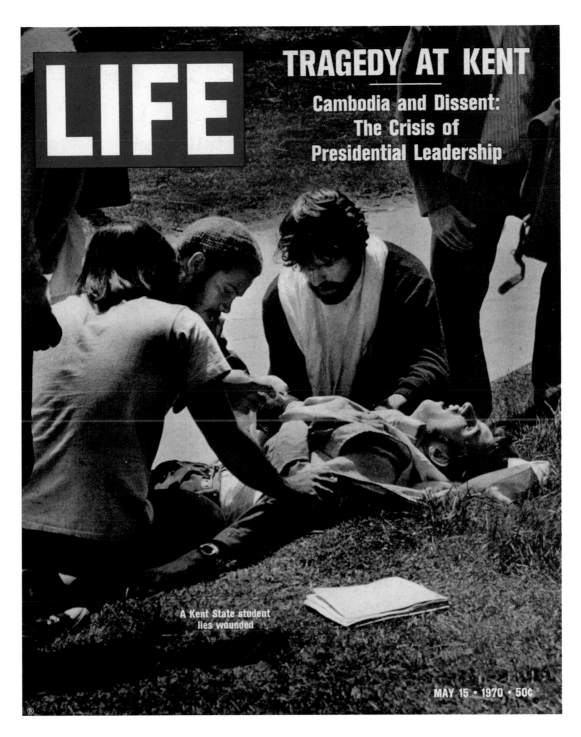

The cover of *Life* magazine shows student Joe Cullum *(center with beard)* kneeling beside wounded student John Cleary after the Ohio National Guard opened fire on Kent State University Vietnam War protestors. The soldiers killed four students.

Antiwar protests put increasing pressure on the Nixon administration to put an end to the war. Nixon was reluctant to abandon South Vietnam to the Communists. In June 1969, Nixon unveiled a policy called Vietnamization, which provided for the gradual withdrawal of American troops from Vietnam. The troops would be replaced by a greater number of South Vietnamese soldiers. On November 3 of that year, he told the nation, "For the future of peace, precipitate withdrawal would . . . be a disaster of immense magnitude . . . Our defeat . . . in South Vietnam without question would promote recklessness in the councils of those great powers who have not yet abandoned their goals of world conquest." These "great powers" were the Soviet Union and China, both of which were Communist countries.

Many people think that had Robert Kennedy been elected president in 1968, the war in Vietnam

The single word "shame" was broadcast for two and a half hours on WPIX-TV in New York City because "shame is what everybody should be feeling" about the assassination of Robert F. Kennedy, according to Robert M. Thrower, then president of the station.

would have ended much sooner, probably no later than the spring of 1969. As it happened, the war went on for four more years. An early end would likely have saved tens of thousands of American lives, not to mention several times more Vietnamese lives. As it turns out, the legacy of Bobby Kennedy consists of not only what he left us but also what his assassination robbed us of and left in its stead.

Footnotes

The Ambassador Hotel was once a hot spot for some of Hollywood's most glamorous stars. Ever since it opened in 1921, its famous nightclub, the Cocoanut Grove, had attracted many Hollywood performers, including Barbra Streisand. It was also the site for some of the early Academy Award presentations. The Ambassador has been closed for more than ten years.

Today, it awaits an uncertain fate as investors want to tear it down to build other commercial enterprises. In the meantime, hundreds of movie productions film their location work there. The kitchen pantry where Bobby was shot, however, is boarded up and off-limits to visitors in an effort to prevent vandalism and deter souvenir seekers.

Plenty of physical reminders of the assassination still exist, however. In 1998, after thirty years, the Los Angeles Police Department finally released to the public all records, photographs, videotapes, and other evidence from the Kennedy assassination. All of this evidence is stored at the state archives in California's capital, Sacramento. The physical evidence includes the shirt that Sirhan wore on the night of the shooting and the gun that he used. The release of these materials was in part due to the efforts of some dedicated private citizens who felt that it was important for the public to have access to this information.

There is also a private collection of assassination materials at the University of Massachusetts Dartmouth Library, called, appropriately, the Robert F. Kennedy Assassination Archives. As these institutions preserve Kennedy's memory, we, too, must remember his legacy as a leader who fought for social justice. Ultimately, whatever the truth, Kennedy's assassination serves as a grim reminder of the responsibility we all share to ensure that the government and its representatives should not and must not keep secrets from the people.

Changing Times

May 1954
The U.S. Supreme Court rules against racial segregation in public schools in *Brown v. Board of Education*.

November 1960
John F. Kennedy is elected president of the United States.

April 1961
The Bay of Pigs invasion is launched to overthrow the newly established Communist regime in Cuba headed by Fidel Castro.

May 1961
Freedom Riders set out on bus trips across the South to challenge segregation on buses and in bus stations; in September, segregation is finally made unlawful.

October 1962
James Meredith, the first black student to enroll at the University of Mississippi, registers after 20,000 federal troops are called in to maintain order on campus.

November 1963
President John F. Kennedy is assassinated in Dallas, Texas.

July 1964
The Civil Rights Act passes.

August 1964
The USS *Maddox* is attacked by North Vietnamese in the Gulf of Tonkin.

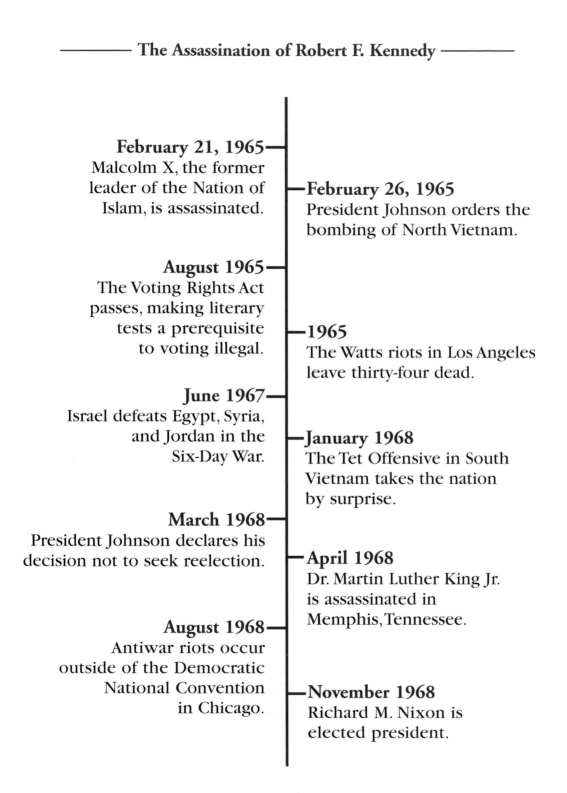

The Assassination of Robert F. Kennedy

February 21, 1965
Malcolm X, the former leader of the Nation of Islam, is assassinated.

February 26, 1965
President Johnson orders the bombing of North Vietnam.

August 1965
The Voting Rights Act passes, making literary tests a prerequisite to voting illegal.

1965
The Watts riots in Los Angeles leave thirty-four dead.

June 1967
Israel defeats Egypt, Syria, and Jordan in the Six-Day War.

January 1968
The Tet Offensive in South Vietnam takes the nation by surprise.

March 1968
President Johnson declares his decision not to seek reelection.

April 1968
Dr. Martin Luther King Jr. is assassinated in Memphis, Tennessee.

August 1968
Antiwar riots occur outside of the Democratic National Convention in Chicago.

November 1968
Richard M. Nixon is elected president.

Glossary

agenda Plan of things to do.

autopsy Medical exam conducted on a dead person to find out the cause of death.

blacklist To put someone on a list of people who are to be avoided.

caricature Cartoon drawing of a person in which some recognizable physical feature is exaggerated to produce a comical effect.

commute To change or alter; to give in exchange.

conspiracy Secret plan involving a group of people.

delegates Representatives at the nominating conventions who vote on behalf of the voters.

delinquency Failure to do what one is supposed to do, often referring to students who drop out of school.

detractor Person who seeks to belittle his or her opponent.

evidentiary hearing Meeting outside of the actual trial to examine the evidence of a case.

guerrilla tactics Plan of military attacks that uses the element of surprise to overcome the enemy.

hypnosis Method of controlling the thoughts and actions of a person by making suggestions to his or her subconscious.

incumbent Person who is currently holding a political office.

jurisdiction Power to rule over someone or something.

manifest destiny A future event accepted as inevitable.

primary Election where the voters choose the candidates who will run for office.

print journalists Reporters who work for the printed media, such as newspapers and magazines, as opposed to television or radio.

prosecute To bring to justice in a court of law.

slander False rumor about a person that makes him or her look bad.

vandalism Deliberate destruction of property.

For More Information

Organizations

Assassination Archive and Research Center (AARC)
918 F Street NW, Room 510
Washington, DC 20004
(202) 393-1917

Citizens for Truth about the Kennedy Assassinations (CTKA)
P.O. Box 5489
Sherman Oaks, CA 91413
(310) 838-9494

Coalition on Political Assassinations (COPA)
P. O. Box 772
Ben Franklin Station
Washington, DC 20044-0772
(202) 785-5299

The Conspiracy Museum
110 South Market Street
Dallas, TX 75202
(214) 741-3040

Robert F. Kennedy Assassination Archives
University of Massachusetts Dartmouth Library
285 Old Westport Road
North Dartmouth, MA 02747-2300
(508) 999-8680
Web site: http://www.lib.umassd.edu

Web Sites

The Robert F. Kennedy Assassination
http://homepages.tcp.co.uk/~dlewis

Simple Facts About the Robert F. Kennedy Assassination
http://flag.blackened.net/daver/misc/rfk.html

Who Killed Bobby Kennedy?
http://www.daywilliams.com/kennedy_bobby.html

Works Cited

Cassidy, Sheila L., ed., *Remembering Jack and Bobby: A Kennedy Anthology.* Sedona, AZ: In Print Publishing, 1992.

Newfield, Jack. *Robert Kennedy; A Memoir.* New York: Plume, 1969.

http://www.rfkmemorial.org/RFK/rfk_quotes.htm

For Further Reading

Cassidy, Sheila L., ed. *Remembering Jack and Bobby:
A Kennedy Anthology.* Sedona, AZ: In Print
Publishing, 1992.

Harrison, Barbara, and Daniel Terris. *A Ripple of
Hope: The Life of Robert F. Kennedy.* New York:
Lodestar Books, 1997.

Mills, Judie. *Robert Kennedy.* Brookfield, CT:
Millbrook Press, 1998.

Murphy, Tom. *Jack and Bobby.* New York:
MetroBooks, 1998.

Petrillo, Daniel J. *Robert F. Kennedy.* World Leaders
Past and Present. New York: Chelsea House, 1989.

Santella, Andrew. *The Assassination of Robert F.
Kennedy.* Cornerstones of Freedom. Danbury, CT:
Children's Press, 1998.

Schoor, Gene. *Young Robert Kennedy.* New York:
McGraw-Hill, 1969.

Index

Index

About the Author

Juliet Ching lives on the West Coast with her family and pets. She is a freelance copy editor and writer.

Photo Credits

Cover © Bill Epperidge/Timepix; p. 1 © Discovery Channel/AP; pp. 4, 6, 7, 15, 17, 19, 35, 40, 52 © Bettmann/Corbis; p. 11, 13, 24, 41 © AP/Wide World Photos; p. 20 © Hulton/Archive; p. 27 © Ted Streshinsky/Corbis; pp. 28, 51 © Time Inc.; p. 32 © Vittoriano Rastelli/Corbis; p. 42 © California State Archives; p. 49 © Lee Balterman/Timepix.

Series Design and Layout

Les Kanturek